Welcome to the enchanting of the Flowers Coloring Book.

Thank you from the bottom of our hearts for choosing our Flowers coloring book! We hope each page blooms with joy as you bring your creativity to life through vibrant colors. May this book be a source of relaxation and inspiration, turning every stroke into a masterpiece. Happy coloring!

ARTINK
PUBLISHING

THIS BOOK BELONGS TO

Dear buyer!

Hope you're having fun with your new coloring book! If you've reached the end, I'm assuming you enjoyed it.

I wanted to chat with you about something important – your thoughts. The idea of asking for reviews didn't hit me right away. But as I thought more about it, I realized that happy customers often don't leave reviews, while those who didn't vibe with the book might be more vocal.

I'm committed to ensuring my coloring books are fairly evaluated, and your feedback is essential to achieving that.

To leave a review, simply scan the QR code below with your smartphone camera. It will take you directly to the Amazon review page for the coloring book you purchased.

Best regards,
Artink Publishing Team.